LIVING THINGS

ROBERT SNEDDEN

Bird

FRANKLIN WATTS
LONDON•SYDNEY

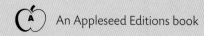 An Appleseed Editions book

First published in 2007 by Franklin Watts
338 Euston Road, London NW1 3BH

Franklin Watts Australia
Hachette Children's Books
Level 17/207 Kent St, Sydney, NSW 2000

© 2007 Appleseed Editions

Created by Appleseed Editions Ltd,
Well House, Friars Hill, Guestling,
East Sussex TN35 4ET

Designed by Guy Callaby
Edited by Pip Morgan
Illustrations by Guy Callaby
Picture research by Su Alexander

ISBN 978 07496 7551 6

Dewey Classification: 598

A CIP catalogue for this book is available from the British Library.

Picture acknowledgements

Title page Doug Wechsler/Nature Picture Library; 3 Hanne & Jens Eriksen/Nature Picture
Library; 4 Tony Heald/Nature Picture Library; 5l Pete Oxford/Nature Picture Library, r Eric
Baccega/Nature Picture Library; 7t Galen Rowell/Corbis, b Colin Seddon/Nature Picture
Library; 8 Bernard Castelein/Nature Picture Library; 9 Darrell Gulin/Corbis; 10 Jeff Vanuga/
Corbis; 11 Doug Allan/Nature Picture Library; 12 Tony Heald/Nature Picture Library;
14 Dave Watts/Nature Picture Library; 15 Adam White/Nature Picture Library; 17t Pete
Oxford/Nature Picture Library, b Jeff Foott/Nature Picture Library; 18 David Kjaer/Nature
Picture Library; 19t Rolf Nussbaumer/Nature Picture Library, b Pete Oxford/Nature Picture
Library; 20 Doug Wechsler/Nature Picture Library; 21t Bengt Lundberg/Nature Picture
Library b Eric Hosking/Corbis; 22 Horst Ossinger/DPA/Corbis; 23t Phil Savoie/Nature
Picture Library, b Barry Mansell/Nature Picture Library; 24 Kim Taylor/Nature Picture
Library; 25 Brian Lightfoot/Nature Picture Library; 26 Colin Seddon/Nature Picture Library;
27t Rolf Nussbaumer/Nature Picture Library, b Hanne & Jens Eriksen/Nature Picture
Library; 28 Tom Mangelsen/Nature Picture Library; 29 Frank Lukasseck/ZEFA/Corbis:

Front cover W.Perry Conway/Corbis

Printed in China

Contents

What is a bird?

You probably have a pretty good idea what a bird is already. We share the world with many wild animals, but birds are usually the ones we see and hear most. Even in the hearts of our cities there are birds, whether they be flocks of pigeons or the occasional hawk. We keep birds as pets and we eat many of them as food.

A riot of birds

Birds come in a wide variety of shapes, sizes and colours. From elegant pink flamingoes and waddling penguins, to soaring eagles and noisily squawking parrots, birds make the world a noisier and more colourful place. They are all different and yet they are all birds.

BELOW
Lammergeiers live in the mountains of southern Europe and Africa. They drop bones from a great height to crack them open so they can eat the marrow inside.

The smallest bird in the world is the bee hummingbird, which is just over six centimetres long and weighs less than two grams. The heaviest flying bird is the great bustard, which can weigh over 20 kilograms.

LEFT *The cassowary lives in the rainforests of Australia and New Guinea. It can be very dangerous, attacking with its powerful claws.*

ABOVE *This male frigate bird from the Galapagos Islands in the Pacific Ocean attracts the attention of a female by puffing up his bright red throat pouch.*

Eggs and wings

So what makes a bird different from other animals? We might say that a bird is an animal that flies and lays eggs. Bats fly, but they don't lay eggs, so they aren't birds. Penguins don't fly, but they do lay eggs and they are birds. Frogs and fish lay eggs, but they definitely aren't birds. Alligators make nests for their eggs, but they aren't birds, either.

What makes a bird a bird then, and not something else? This book will help you to find out about the remarkable living creatures we call birds. You'll discover some of the things they have in common with other animals – and just what it is that makes them special.

Birds and feathers

Birds are the only animals that have feathers. Quite simply, if an animal has feathers, then it is a bird.

All birds, from parrots to penguins, have feathers. A bird's feathers are very important. They keep it warm and dry and help to cushion its body from injury. Feathers may be camouflaged to hide the bird from predators or specially coloured to attract a mate. Without feathers no bird could fly.

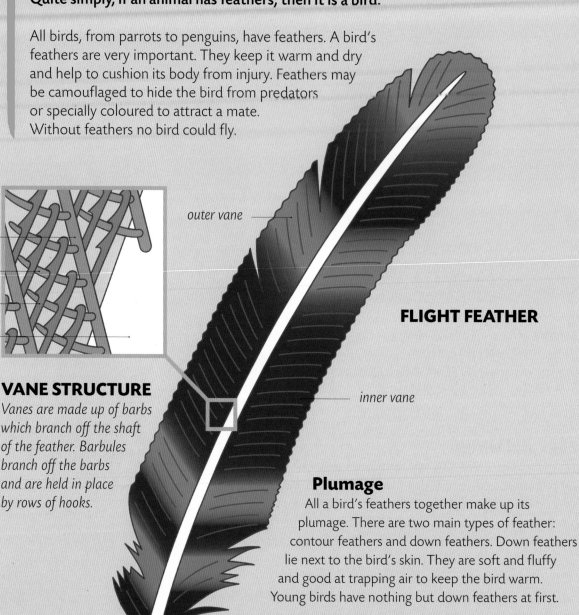

barb

barbule

hook

shaft

outer vane

FLIGHT FEATHER

inner vane

shaft

VANE STRUCTURE
Vanes are made up of barbs which branch off the shaft of the feather. Barbules branch off the barbs and are held in place by rows of hooks.

Plumage
All a bird's feathers together make up its plumage. There are two main types of feather: contour feathers and down feathers. Down feathers lie next to the bird's skin. They are soft and fluffy and good at trapping air to keep the bird warm. Young birds have nothing but down feathers at first.

As a bird grows older it begins to grow contour feathers. Contour feathers look flat and smooth. They are arranged in regular rows on the body and overlap each other so there are no gaps between them. The contour feathers are the ones that give the bird its shape and also its colour. Specially shaped contour feathers called flight feathers make up the bird's wings and tail and enable it to fly.

Feather structure

Feathers are made from the same material as the scales of a reptile, and your nails and hair. This is a strong, lightweight and flexible substance called keratin. A hollow central shaft runs down the middle of each feather and attaches it to the bird's body. The softer vanes of the feather grow out in two rows on either side of the shaft.

On the contour feathers many tiny hooks fasten the vanes together, keeping the feather flat and smooth. Down feathers don't have these hooks so they stay fluffy.

RIGHT *This young king penguin chick is beginning to lose its downy juvenile feathers as it gains its adult plumage.*

LEFT *The speckled breast of this Mauritius kestrel clearly shows how the contour feathers neatly overlap each other.*

WOW!

The longest feathers ever seen were on a chicken in Japan. Its tail feathers measured 10.59 metres long! The bird with most feathers is the whistling swan, which has around 25,000.

Feather care

A bird couldn't survive long without its feathers. So it takes great care of them and keeps them in good condition.

Preening

Feathers, particularly the contour feathers of the wings, need to be kept smooth and flat and in the right place. The bird does this by running its beak along the feathers and nibbling at the edges. This is called preening. It helps to rid the feathers of any dirt and also makes sure that the tiny hooks linking the feather vanes together are all joined up properly.

Many birds can also waterproof their feathers. They have a preen gland near their tail. This produces an oily substance that the bird spreads over its feathers while it is preening. The oil also helps to keep the feathers flexible.

BELOW *The kingfisher takes particular care to waterproof its feathers to prevent it becoming waterlogged when it dives to catch a fish.*

Powder down

Birds that don't have preen glands grow special feathers called powder down on their breasts. These feathers grow all the time. Their tips break down into a fine waterproof powder that the bird spreads over its feathers in the same way as other birds use oil from their preen gland. Water birds, such as egrets and herons, have large amounts of powder down. Most birds have some, even those with preen glands.

Moulting

No amount of care can stop feathers from wearing out or being damaged. Birds regularly lose old feathers and replace them with new ones. This is called moulting. The old feathers are pushed out by the new ones growing beneath them. A small bird may change its feathers in a month or two, but a large bird such as an eagle may take a few years to completely change its plumage.

ABOVE *The great egret collects powder down from its breast. It will use this to waterproof its feathers.*

WOW!

Water birds, such as ducks and swans, lose their flight feathers all at once. They can't fly for several weeks until the new feathers grow.

Wings – but not to fly

There is one thing all birds have in common. They have wings. Birds' wings come in a variety of shapes and sizes. Most birds use their wings for one very obvious purpose – to fly. Some birds, however, never leave the ground, but they still use their wings.

An ostrich running at full speed over the African grasslands is almost impossible to catch!

Big birds

The biggest birds in the world can't fly. They include the emu from Australia, the rhea from South America and the biggest of all, the African ostrich. The ostrich is an impressive animal at nearly 2.5 metres tall and weighing over 130 kilograms. It would take a mighty big pair of wings to get an ostrich off the ground.

These big birds have given up flying. Instead, they have long and powerful legs that allow them to run at remarkable speeds. An ostrich, for example, can reach 70 kilometres an hour, fast enough to leave most predators behind. As they run they spread out their stubby wings, which act like stabilisers and help them to keep their balance.

Flying underwater

Penguins are birds that have given up the air and taken to the water. Like ostriches and emus, they are not built for flying, but neither are they built for running. A torpedo-shaped penguin may look amusing as it waddles over the snow, but it is just the right shape for moving smoothly through water. It really comes into its own when it takes to the ocean. A penguin's wings are called flippers, and are shorter and harder than those of flying birds. They are shaped like paddles and are very useful for speeding through the water.

ABOVE *Emperor penguins are the champion divers of the bird world. They can reach depths of 500 metres in search of food. The greatest depth ever reached by a human without breathing equipment is 172 metres.*

Kiwis and kakapos

New Zealand is home to two of the world's most unusual birds. The chicken-sized kiwi is a shy and secretive forest dweller. It has very small wings and no tail at all. During the day, kiwis hide in burrows or under logs, emerging at night to eat berries and bugs on the forest floor. They might not be able to fly, but they can outrun most humans!

The kakapo is a rather special bird. It is the world's heaviest parrot, weighing up to four kilograms. It is the only parrot in the world that is active at night and the only parrot that can't fly. It is also the world's rarest parrot – there are fewer than a hundred left. Kakapos are good climbers and use their wings to balance in the branches.

Built for flight

Most birds are built to fly and to spend at least some of their lives in the air. All birds have a pair of wings instead of front legs or arms and a flying bird has powerful breast muscles, light bones, big lungs and a large heart.

Lift-off!

Taking to the air requires a lot of strength. When a bird takes off it has to lift itself into the air by sheer muscle power. Birds have powerful breast muscles to give themselves that first strong beat of the wings which lifts them off the ground. The breast muscles of birds such as pigeons can make up a third of the bird's total weight.

Pumping power

Just like your heart, a bird's heart pumps oxygen-rich blood around the body to where it is needed. A bird's heart is big and strong, and has a structure similar to a mammal's heart. In relation to its body weight, a bird's heart is bigger than a mammal's.

An African fish eagle swoops down from a tree to snatch a fish from the water, then lifts into the air with its powerful wings.

BIRD SKELETON

A bird's skeleton has several adaptations for flight, including a light skull without teeth or heavy jawbones, a wishbone to support the wings and a large sternum to anchor the big flight muscles.

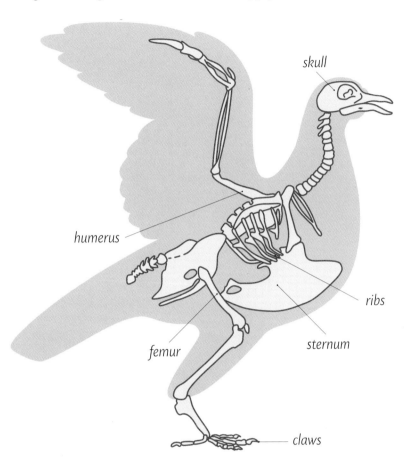

skull

humerus

ribs

femur

sternum

claws

Hollow bones

Weight is an important factor in flying. The heavier the bird, the more power it needs to fly. Birds are adapted to weigh as little as possible. They have very light, hollow bones and do not have many of the bones that other animals have. The skeletons of some birds actually weigh less than their feathers do!

What's that splat?

Birds also weigh less because they do not have bladders to store urine. Rather than producing liquid urine to get rid of wastes, birds produce a white paste-like substance. That's what a bird dropping is!

Air supply

Flying takes a lot of energy – much more than walking or running. This means that a bird needs a good supply of oxygen to help it release energy from food. A bird's lungs are much more complicated and efficient than those of mammals, such as us. They also take up much more space in a bird's body. Your lungs fill about a twentieth of your body but a bird's fill about a fifth.

BIRD RESPIRATORY SYSTEM

As well as two lungs, birds have nine air sacs – five at the front and four at the rear. Some of the front sacs are inside hollow bones.

The bird breathes in through the trachea to fill the rear air sacs with fresh, oxygen-rich air. This air is then squeezed from the rear air sacs into the lungs. Oxygen passes from the lungs into the bloodstream, leaving behind stale air. The stale air then moves from the lungs into the front air sacs. Finally, the bird breathes it out of the front air sacs through the trachea.

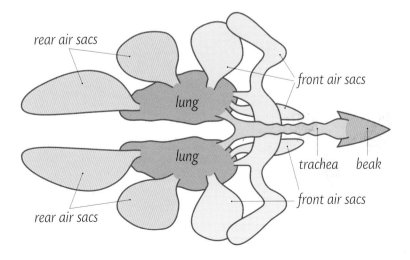

rear air sacs

front air sacs

lung

lung

trachea   beak

rear air sacs

front air sacs

Wings to fly

Once a bird has propelled itself up into the air it has to stay there. So what stops a bird from simply fluttering back down to the ground again?

Lift and drag

Take a sheet of paper and hold it loosely by the edge so that it flops down in front of you. Now blow hard across the top of the paper (not underneath it). Watch how the air flowing across the paper makes it rise. The air flowing over the paper results in an upward force called lift.

Birds and aeroplanes both stay up in the air by creating lift. A bird creates lift by flapping its wings to make the air flow over them. The engines of an aeroplane create lift by pushing it forwards and forcing the air to flow over its wings.

Air doesn't just keep the bird up, however. Air resistance also slows the bird down as it flies forwards. This is called drag. A bird's wings are shaped to cut as smoothly as possible through the air. The bird also holds its wings at an angle to make sure that it gets as much lift as possible.

Hovering hummingbirds

Hummingbirds can hover in one spot. A hovering hummingbird has no air flowing over its wings to give lift. Instead it keeps itself up by beating its wings very rapidly forwards and backwards. Its wings twist around so they are always pushing the bird upwards. By tilting its wings a hummingbird can fly in any direction. It can even fly upside down for a second or two!

The broad-billed hummingbird is a frequent summer visitor to gardens in the south-west of the USA.

BIRD WING

A bird's wing is made up of primary and secondary feathers with smaller feathers called coverts covering where the primaries attach to the wing.

Primaries

Secondaries

Primary coverts

Secondary coverts

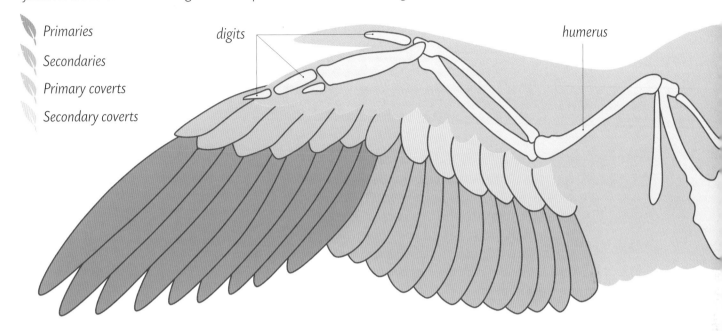

digits

humerus

Primaries and secondaries

The feathers that make up a bird's wing are not all the same. Primary feathers propel the bird through the air. Usually, birds have ten of these primaries on each wing. They are attached to bones that, in humans, would be the hand. If a bird's primaries are lost or damaged it is unable to fly.

Secondary wing feathers are attached to bones that would be the forearm in humans. Secondaries shape the wing into an ideal surface for flying and form the main surface which air flows over, giving lift.

WOW!

The wandering albatross has the longest wings in the world. Some have wingspans of over 3.5 metres. The highest flying bird is the griffon vulture. In 1973 one collided with an aeroplane more than 11,000 metres above the Ivory Coast in Africa.

Bird digestion

Birds use a lot of energy, which means they need a lot of food. When they're awake, most birds spend much of their time looking for something to eat. Many birds consume a fifth of their body weight in food every day to get the energy they need. Imagine how you'd feel if you had to eat that much.

Crop storage

When you swallow your food it goes down a tube and into your stomach. In birds, this tube has an enlarged section called the crop where food can be stored for later if the stomach is full. A bird can also use its crop to carry food to its chicks. Another advantage is that the crop allows a bird to feed swiftly and then fly to a safe place to digest its meal.

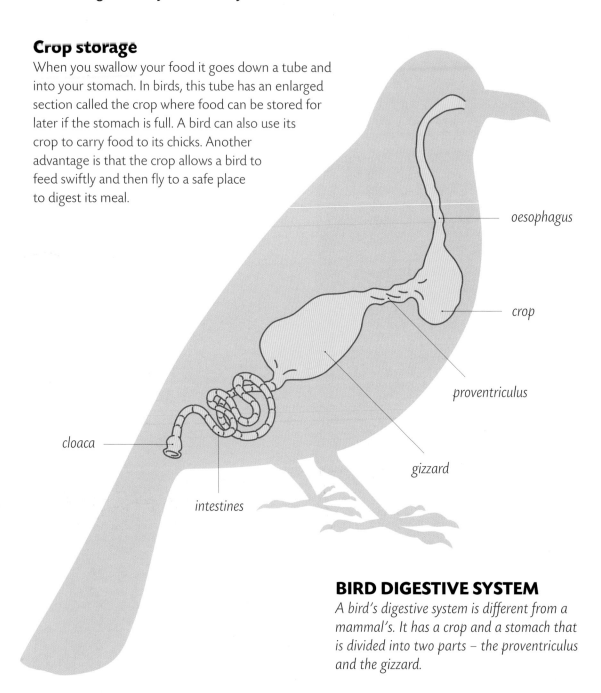

oesophagus

crop

proventriculus

gizzard

intestines

cloaca

BIRD DIGESTIVE SYSTEM

A bird's digestive system is different from a mammal's. It has a crop and a stomach that is divided into two parts – the proventriculus and the gizzard.

Grinding gizzards

Birds have no teeth and so cannot chew their food. They must either swallow it whole or use their beak to crack or tear it into pieces. A two-part stomach helps a bird's digestive process.

The first part of the stomach begins to break down the food using digestive juices. The second part, or gizzard, has very powerful muscles that grind up the bird's food. To get an idea how powerful the gizzard is, try squashing a walnut shell between your fingers. A turkey's gizzard is strong enough to crush it! Sometimes birds swallow small stones that stay in the gizzard, helping the grinding process.

Birds of prey use their gizzards to store indigestible parts of their catch, such as bones and fur. This becomes a pellet that the bird eventually spits out.

End of the line

Once the food has been pulverised and dissolved by the stomach it passes into the intestines. From here, all the nutrients from the food are absorbed into the bloodstream and transported to the rest of the bird's body. Your intestines work in much the same way. The bird's digestive system ends at the cloaca. Here, anything left over that couldn't be digested is stored before being expelled.

RIGHT *Owls spit out pellets of indigestible bone, fur and other material. We can learn a lot about the owl's diet by looking at these pellets.*

Bills and beaks

A bird doesn't have arms and hands to help it lift or carry something. If it wants to pick up anything It has to use its feet or its bill. Is it a bill or is it a beak? There's no difference really, they're just two words for the same thing.

Almost all the work of feeding is done by the bill and looking at a bird's bill tells you a lot about the sort of food it eats. For instance, hummingbirds have long beaks to reach the nectar in flowers, like drinking through a straw. Woodpeckers have bills like sharp chisels that they use to chip away at tree trunks to find insects hiding there. Ducks and flamingoes have bills that strain tiny animals and plant material out of water.

BELOW *The strong, hooked bill of the common buzzard marks it out as a predator that is able to tear strips from its prey.*

Bills and jaws

A bird's bill is not the same thing as another animal's jaws. The bill is actually a horny covering over the bird's jaw. Birds have very light jaws compared with those of reptiles and mammals. This is another way that birds save weight and so make flying easier.

Swiss Army bills

A bird's bill has to do many things – a bit like a Swiss Army knife! As well as eating food it might catch food, probe for it, dig for it, scoop it from water or carry it to the nest. Birds use their bills to look after their feathers, to fetch materials for their nests and to defend themselves. At the start of their lives they use their bills to peck through the eggshell and into the world.

BELOW *The flamingo collects tiny plants and animals from the water by pumping the water back out through slits in its beak and bristles on its tongue.*

Hunting and fishing

Hunting birds, such as hawks and eagles, have strong beaks that are thick and curved with sharp hooks that they use to tear at their prey. Herons and egrets have long, spear-like beaks that they use to catch fish. Pelicans dive under water and scoop up fish in the bottom part of their big beaks, like catching them in a net.

Seed eaters

Seed-eating birds, such as sparrows and finches, have hard, cone-shaped beaks that can vary a great deal. Some birds eat tiny seeds and have small bills to match. Others have heavy bills combined with powerful jaw muscles that can crack big seeds such as cherry stones.

ABOVE *A curlew uses its long bill to probe beneath the surface of mudflats for small animals to eat.*

WOW!

The Australian pelican has the longest bill in the world. It is nearly half a metre in length. The sword-billed hummingbird, with its ten-centimetre long bill, is the only bird with a bill that's longer than its body.

Songs and calls

One of the first things that might spring to mind when you think about birds is their singing. Not all birds sing and some sing more pleasantly than others to our ears. When a bird sings it has far more important things than our pleasure in mind.

I'm here!

Birds call and sing to communicate with other birds. Among songbirds the male sings most often. One of the things he is saying is, "This is my place. You stay away!" He is telling other birds of the same kind that this is his territory. In spring, males also hope to attract a mate with their singing.

BELOW *A male western meadowlark sings out – perhaps to attract a mate, warn off rivals, or both! The bird spends summer in North America and flies south in winter.*

The voice box

Near the top of your throat is your larynx, or voice box. When you speak or sing this vibrates to produce different sounds. The voice box of a bird is called a syrinx. It is shaped like an upside down Y and located at the bottom end of its throat. Here it splits to join the lungs so there are two parts that vibrate to make sound. This means that the bird has two different sound sources rather than just the one we have. The two sources blend together producing a complex variety of sounds.

Not all birds have a syrinx, and some have a syrinx that is undeveloped. For example, some vultures don't have one and can only make various hissing and grunting noises.

The language of birds

Most birds have a number of calls they use to send messages to one another. There are many reasons why birds call. A hungry chick in the nest will call to its parents to be fed. In a large seabird colony a returning parent can find its own chick by recognising its call. Chicks also have distress calls that they make to alert their parents to danger.

Birds that fly in flocks communicate with each other by calling. A flocking call can bring a scattered group of birds back together again, for example.

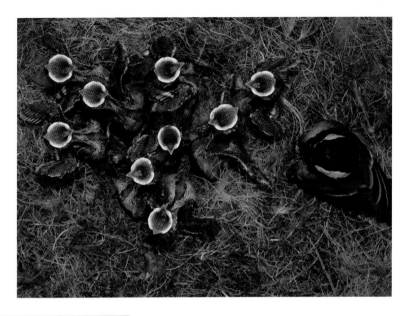

ABOVE *Chicks, such as these great tits, call out to get attention when a parent returns with food.*

LEFT *When a flock of California quails are feeding, one will stand guard ready to give a loud call to alert the other birds to any danger.*

WOW!

The song of a European wren is made up of more than 700 different notes a minute and can be heard more than 500 metres away.

Look at me!

Some birds are rather drab and dull. Others appear very bright and colourful. Sometimes we see these differences in the same kind of bird. The male birds draw attention to themselves with their showy feathers while the females are much more plain. What is the reason for this?

Breeding plumage

Very often the reason the male is so brightly coloured is to try to attract the attention of a mate. The message here is, "Look at me! See how fit and healthy I am." The male birds with the brightest, most spectacular plumage are the ones that are most attractive to the females.

At the same time, the male is sending a message to rival males. He is showing them how good he is at defending his territory and his eye-catching visual display is often accompanied by loud singing.

BELOW *The contrast between the bright blue male peacock with his immense tail and the drab brown female peahen is extraordinary.*

LEFT *An exotic male Raggiana bird of paradise displays in front of a smaller female on the right. The female has to build the nest and look after the young by herself.*

A male bird trying to attract a female risks attracting the attentions of a predator, too. However, some males don't seem to care. One example is the group known as birds of paradise, which are members of the crow family. The males are, perhaps, the most colourful birds on the planet. While showing off their bright plumage they cry raucously and perform vigorous dances on the forest floor. Definitely attention grabbers!

Camouflage nesting

Female birds usually take care of the eggs in the nest. It wouldn't be a good idea for the female to draw the attention of hunting animals to herself and her eggs. A brightly-coloured female would be much easier to see than a drab one. The female's feathers help to camouflage her by blending in with the background and making her difficult to see. When the chicks hatch they are coloured like their mother for the same reason.

ABOVE *This Wilson's plover and its eggs are both well camouflaged in its shoreline habitat in Key Largo, Florida.*

A young bird's drab plumage doesn't just help to keep it hidden. If dad happens to visit the nest it tells him that the chick is harmless, and not a competing rival that has to be attacked and driven away.

Egg laying

All female birds lay eggs. They are not the only animals to lay eggs, of course. Insects, fish, amphibians and reptiles all lay eggs, too. But birds look after their eggs better than most others.

If all eight of these great tit eggs hatch the parents will have to work very hard to keep the hungry chicks properly fed.

Life support

A bird's egg is like a chick's life-support system. It provides both food and protection for the growing young bird inside. The eggshell contains calcium, a substance also found in bones. Female birds have a special kind of bone that they use to store the calcium they need for their eggs. It takes about 15 hours for a hen's egg to form inside her body.

Eggshells are waterproof but not airproof. Thousands of tiny holes in the shell let air pass back and forth so the chick inside receives the oxygen it needs and waste gases can escape. Inside the egg, there is a yellow yolk surrounded by clear egg white, or albumen. The yolk is the chick's food supply. The albumen acts like a cushion to protect the chick. It is also a source of water.

Why lay eggs?

There is a good reason why birds lay eggs rather than give birth to live young. Birds often lay several eggs over a period of a few days. If she had to carry her growing young inside her, a female bird would find it hard to get off the ground, making her vulnerable to predators. Another advantage of eggs is that the father can share in caring for them, although not all bird fathers do!

The number of eggs varies from one bird to another. A giant albatross, for example, lays one egg every other year. If conditions are good and food is plentiful a European blackbird may lay a clutch of five eggs four times in one year.

ABOVE *The young chick has to peck its way out of the egg when it is ready to hatch. Here, a young lesser black-backed gull is about to make an appearance on May Island in Scotland.*

WOW!

The world's smallest bird eggs are those of the vervain hummingbird, weighing just over a third of a gram. The ostrich lays the biggest eggs, which weigh about 1.5 kilograms each. The champion egg layer, however, is the kiwi. Her eggs are a quarter of her own weight – that would be the equivalent of an ostrich laying a 40-kilogram egg!

*Ostrich egg
18 cm tall x 14 cm wide*

*Vervain hummingbird egg
1.3 cm tall x 0.8 cm wide*

Nest building

Most birds make nests to protect their eggs from bad weather and predators. The amount of work that goes into making the nest varies from one type of bird to another.

Scrape nests

A scrape nest is just what it sounds like – a hollow in the ground scraped out by the bird. Some birds line their scrapes with sticks or leaves, while others just lay their eggs straight on the ground. Penguins, vultures and shorebirds, such as gulls and terns, all have scrape nests. Eggs in a scrape nest are usually well camouflaged by the markings on their shells.

Burrows and hollows

Some birds, such as kingfishers and puffins, nest in burrows. Some construct their own burrows, while others use burrows abandoned by rabbits or voles.

Many birds, such as woodpeckers, owls and parrots, make their nests in tree holes. The male hornbill actually seals the female inside a tree hole to protect her from predators while she is incubating her eggs. He feeds her through a small slit just big enough for her beak. When the chicks have hatched and are ready to leave the nest the hole is opened up again.

LEFT *A puffin looks out from the safety of its nest burrow in Wales. The burrow is usually about a metre deep and is lined with feathers, grass and leaves.*

Cup nests

When you think of a bird's nest you probably think of a cup nest. This is the most common sort of nest and is made from a variety of materials. Cup nests are usually built above the ground, most often in trees or bushes.

Generally, a bird uses anything it can find to weave its nest. Grass, leaves and twigs are most common, but birds have also used sweet wrappers among other things. A bird lines the inside of the nest with soft materials, such as discarded feathers and bits of animal fur. A hummingbird's nest, the smallest in the world, may be made from spider webs and moss.

LEFT *African weaver birds make complex hanging nests by weaving together blades of grass and other materials.*

ABOVE *Bald eagles, such as this one in Florida, can make huge nests of wood in the branches of trees.*

Bird world

Birds are very remarkable creatures. There are around 9,000 different kinds of bird in the world and they live just about everywhere. They soar in the mountains, raise their chicks in the polar cold, glide over the ocean waves, hunt in the deserts and forests, and sing in our gardens.

Birds range in size from tall ostriches running across the grasslands of Africa to tiny hummingbirds darting from flower to flower in the Americas. In numbers they range from million-strong flocks of queleas – an African finch – to solitary and rare condors.

For millions of years migrating birds, such as these whooping cranes in North Dakota, have criss-crossed the planet in search of feeding grounds and nesting sites.

Birds of a feather

Wherever they live, whatever their size and their habits, all birds have some things in common. They have two legs, two wings and a bill. The females lay eggs. Most importantly, they all have feathers. No other living thing in the world has feathers. These are what make birds unique.

Birds in the world

Like every other living thing birds play their part in the natural world. There are birds that hunt, whether it be for small creatures such as insects or much bigger prey such as snakes and monkeys. And there are birds that are hunted themselves. Many other animals rely on birds and their eggs and chicks for food. Without birds the living world would be out of balance.

The hyacinth macaw is one of the most spectacular, and one of the most endangered, birds of the Amazon rainforest.

Endangered birds

Birds may be able to fly, but they can't escape from every danger. As we humans grow in numbers and demand more space, so other living things find themselves being pushed out.

Over 400 different types of the world's birds are considered to be endangered. For many it may already be too late. The American ivory-billed woodpecker hasn't been seen since 1997, although some believe it still survives somewhere. Others will need considerable help from humans if they are to survive.

Glossary

Adaptation A feature of a living thing that makes it better suited to its particular lifestyle; the ability to fly is an adaptation of most birds.

Albumen The 'white' of an egg surrounding the yolk in the middle; albumen is actually clear and colourless and helps to protect the growing chick.

Calcium A mineral that is a necessary part of living things; it is found in bones, teeth and in the shells of eggs.

Camouflage Colours or patterns on a bird or other animal that make it hard to see against its surroundings.

Cloaca The final part of the bird's digestive system where anything undigested is stored before it is expelled.

Clutch A group of eggs laid in a nest at about the same time.

Contour feathers Smooth, flat feathers that give the bird its shape and colour.

Coverts Small feathers that cover the place where the primary feathers attach to the wing.

Crop Part of a bird's digestive system where food can be stored temporarily.

Display What a male bird does to attract the attentions of a female or to warn off a male rival.

Down feathers Small, soft and fluffy feathers that lie close to the bird's skin and keep it warm.

Drag The force that slows down an object as it travels through the air, caused by friction with the air.

Forage To search for food.

Gizzard A strong and muscular part of a bird's digestive system where food is ground down and broken up; the second part of the bird's two-part stomach (see proventriculus).

Gliding Flying a short distance without flapping the wings.

Incubate To sit on eggs to keep them warm and hatch them.

Keratin A strong, flexible material in feathers, hair, horns and scales.

Lift The upward force that keeps a bird, or an aeroplane, in the air.

Moulting The process by which a bird's old, damaged feathers are replaced with new ones; a complete moult may take from a few weeks to a few years, depending on the bird.

Pellet Indigestible part of a meal, such as fur and bones, that is spat out by birds such as owls.

Powder down A type of very fine down feathers that break up to form a fine powder, like talcum, that birds such as herons and egrets spread over their feathers to help waterproof and clean them.

Plumage All the feathers of a bird.

Preen gland A gland near a bird's tail; it produces oil that the bird uses to waterproof its feathers.

Preening What a bird does to clean and groom its feathers.

Primary feathers The outermost feathers of a bird's wing; these are strong and flexible to propel the bird through the air.

Proventriculus The first part of a bird's two-part stomach, where the process of digestion begins.

Secondary feathers The wing feathers nearest the bird's body; they form a curved surface that provides the lift the bird needs to stay in the air.

Soaring Flying long distances without flapping the wings. Birds that soar use natural air currents, such as warm air rising, to keep them up.

Syrinx A bird's voice box, similar to the vocal cords, or larynx, of humans; the syrinx vibrates and produces the sounds a bird makes when it sings.

Territory The area a bird or other animal lives in and which it will defend from others; many birds sing to announce to others where their territory is.

Trachea Another name for the windpipe that leads from the mouth to the lungs.

Vane The flat part of the feather, growing from either side of the central shaft.

Yolk The yellow part of the egg; it provides food for the chick growing inside.

Websites

www.pbs.org/lifeofbirds/
Website based on the television series *The Life of Birds* presented by David Attenborough; full of fascinating facts about birds and the making of the programme.

www.birds.cornell.edu/AllAboutBirds/
Information on birds and birdwatching in North America.

www.garden-birds.co.uk/birdgallery.htm
A guide to the birds of Great Britain and where to see them.

www.pitt.edu/~dziadosz/
View nesting birds – real-time webcam feeds and updates photographs of birds' nests around the world.

www.learnbirdsongs.com/
Includes audio files of the songs and calls of many common birds of North America.

www.bl.uk/collections/sound-archive/ listentonature/specialinterestlang/ langofbirdscontents.html
British Library's guide to the language of birds with many sound samples to listen to.

Index